Poems From The West Midlands

Edited By Elle Berry

First published in Great Britain in 2019 by:

Young Writers
Remus House
Coltsfoot Drive
Peterborough
PE2 9BF
Telephone: 01733 890066
Website: www.youngwriters.co.uk

All Rights Reserved
Book Design by Spencer Hart
© Copyright Contributors 2019
Softback ISBN 978-1-78988-903-1
Hardback ISBN 978-1-78988-896-6
Printed and bound in the UK by BookPrintingUK
Website: www.bookprintinguk.com
YB0419O

Foreword

Dear Reader,

Are you ready to explore the wonderful delights of poetry?

Young Writers' *Poetry Patrol* gang set out to encourage and ignite the imaginations of 5-7 year-olds as they took their first steps into the magical world of poetry. With **Riddling Rabbit**, **Acrostic Croc** and **Sensory Skunk** on hand to help, children were invited to write an acrostic, sense poem or riddle on any theme, from people to places, animals to objects, food to seasons. *Poetry Patrol* is also a great way to introduce children to the use of poetic expression, including onomatopoeia and similes, repetition and metaphors, acting as stepping stones for their future poetic journey.

All of us here at Young Writers believe in the importance of inspiring young children to produce creative writing, including poetry, and we feel that seeing their own poem in print will keep that creative spirit burning brightly and proudly.

We hope you enjoy reading this wonderful collection as much as we enjoyed reading all the entries.

Contents

Al-Hijrah School, Bordesley Green

Riytal Khalid Abdulhamid Ali (6)   1

Anderton Park Primary School, Sparkhill

Hiba Noor (6)	2
Latifat Darasimi Onakoya (6)	3
Zakariyah Ibn Sheraz (5)	4
Fatimah Ahmed (6)	5
Dyam Yasin (6)	6
Kashan Ali (6)	7
Areeba Iqbal (6)	8
Amelia Uddin (5)	9

Anson CE Primary School, Great Haywood

Lana Richards (7)	10
Jessica Rose Mullins (7)	11
Oscar Stevens (6)	12

Astley CE Primary School, Astley

Ava Rose Hayes (6)	13
Isabelle Colgan (5)	14
Esme Ray (6)	15
Tyler Jones (6)	16
Naomi Harvey (6)	17

Blakesley Hall Primary School, Birmingham

Zahrah Noor (5)	18
Sarah Shinvari (6)	19
Mary Kamara (6)	20
Jeniah Emanuel-Gardener (6)	21
Zoya Hussain	22
Tayyiba Gous (5)	23
Kawthar Nyanzi (6)	24
Mohammad Yousaf (6)	25
Jarrai Drammeh (6)	26
Sania Shabraz (6)	27
Hasan Khan (6)	28
Inaaya Tariq (6)	29
Logan Quinn-Heffernan (6)	30
Khadija Naveed (6)	31
Aahadh Muhammed (6)	32
Wali Mohammad Ghouri (6)	33
Rawdha Nyanzi (6)	34
Anisah Haseeb (5)	35
Jennah Nawaz (5)	36
Darcie-Ann Evans (5)	37
Aleeza Yasin (6)	38
Abdullah Naveed (6) & Delia	39
Sabrene Messeded (6)	40
Abigail Louise Smith (6)	41
Ethan Dolphin (6)	42
Burhaan Nehman Haq (5)	43
Mohammad Azaan (5)	44
Halimah Ali (5)	45

Brownmead Primary Academy, Shard End

Amia Gibson	46
Leilah Khan (7)	47
Ellie-May Ridings (7)	48
Macie Bayliss (7)	49
Serenity Ingram (7)	50
James Smith (7)	51
Lucas Hewitt-Doyle (8)	52
Carter Fletcher (8)	53
Jack A P Murray (7)	54
Scarlett Coniff	55
Hollie Dowie (7)	56
Lamar Al-Karkhe (7)	57
Caden Summers (6)	58
Malik Elshazly (7)	59
Reyhan Mohammed (7)	60
Ethan McAleenan (7)	61
Kiasha Delarami (7)	62
Orson Dell	63
Shareef Ibn Abdul-Kareem (7)	64

Chilwell Croft Academy, Birmingham

Lawi Mohamed (6)	65
Rabia Mahamed (6)	66
Rami Bashir (6)	67
Abdullah Mohammad Abdallah (5)	68
Aisha Abdihalim Ahmed (6)	69
Caia Patterson (6)	70
Elham Alhassan Safianu (6)	71
Hafiza Begum (6)	72
Abdulrahman Musse (6)	73
Anaya Uddin (6)	74
Mikail Thomas (6)	75
Junior Kisibu Kimuolo (6)	76

Earlsdon Primary School, Coventry

Phoebe King (7)	77
Dolly May Wignall (7)	78

William Senaux (6)	79
Rand Alyasin (6)	80
Oliver (7)	81
Eliza Slack (7)	82
Hazel Fawcett (6)	83
Alayna Quayum (6)	84
Tom Smith (6)	85
Dora Wang (6)	86
Almaya Lily Carrott (6)	87

Hanley St Luke's CE (A) Primary School, Hanley

Lorenzo Tushe (7)	88
Sama Sultani (7)	89

Harper Bell SDA School, Birmingham

Ayanna Mambiri	90
Jada Johnson (5)	91
Nasir Muhammad (5)	92
Marcel Baker (5)	93
Ruel Worrell (5)	94
Ashantae Samuels (5)	95
Matthew Deen-Piper (4)	96
Alayah Ward (5)	97
Semi Awoniranye (5)	98
Esther Nealson (5)	99
Tasia-Ray Berryman (5)	100
Jordan Kerr (5)	101
Cienna Thomas (4)	102
Daniella Deen-Piper (4)	103
Fatima (5)	104

Nathaniel Newton Infant School, Hartshill

Alicia Berrow (5)	105
Macie Moss (6)	106
Joseph Dawson (6)	107
Indy Burbury (6)	108
Aaron Gabriel Szanto (6)	109
Archie Brown (6)	110

Archie Jennings (6)	111
Harry Dunbar (5)	112
Ellie Gabrielle Malkin (6)	113
Callum Cullen (6)	114
Archie Hargreaves (6)	115
Jackson Dudley (6)	116
Saiya Patel (6)	117
George Thomas Weaver (6)	118
Bentley Smalley (6)	119
Stanley Deuster (6)	120
Jack Dani Luke Flannery (5)	121
Jaden Charters (6)	122
Khloé Mullis (5)	123
Harry Robert Wright (6)	124
David Lukash-Alexeenko (6)	125
Georgina Whale (6)	126
Charlie Bliss (6)	127
Carly Underwood (6)	128
George Dyde (6)	129
Shannon Bullock (6)	130
Millie Johnston (6)	131
Harshaan Singh Gill (6)	132
Nedas Jonikas (6)	133
Kai Piff (6)	134
Layla Rose Yates (6)	135
Juan Martinez (6)	136
Marnie Hughes (6)	137
Hadley Hemmings (6)	138
Luke Britton (5)	139
Steven-Junior Bliss (6)	140
Annabelle Wood (7)	141
Alfie Wayne Austin (6)	142
Hollie May Gibson (6)	143
Corey Malyon (6)	144
Keira White (5)	145
Maisie-Lynne Franklin (6)	146
Ralph Oliver Baker (6)	147
Jack Maxie Dodds (6)	148
Oliver Astley (6)	149
Lewis Stevens (6)	150
Ruben Darlison (5)	151
Logan Vaughan Bound (6)	152

Nelson Primary School, Birmingham

Georgia Smith (7)	153
Ankhang Nguyen (7)	154
Mohtady Bashir (7)	156
Lilja Teern (6)	157
Kanyon Armstrong (6)	158
Rayyan Ahmed (6)	159

Our Lady & St Oswald's Catholic Primary School, Oswestry

Constance Harper Denton (6)	160
Alexandra Ali (6)	161
Herbie Brook Jones (6)	162
Isabella Bentley (6)	163
Arrabella Lucia Judd (6)	164
Lottie Grayston (6)	165
Ethan Jeremy Chavez (5)	166
Kieron George Rhodes Chander Owen (7)	167
Buddy Thomas (6)	168
William Abercrombie (7)	169

Perry Hall Primary School, Wednesfield

Freddie Holdcroft (6)	170

Rushall Primary School, Rushall

Bella Gooding (5)	171
Fletcher Christopher Kendrick (5)	172
Mason Smith (6)	174
Mia Stephenson (6)	175
Wyatt Smith (5)	176
Jayden Austin (6)	177
Rosie-Mae (7)	178

St Catherine Of Siena RC Primary School, Lee Bank

Maximilian Schielke (7)	179
Abigail Amanuel (7)	180

St Edward's Catholic Primary School, Selly Park

Eduardo Banito (6)	181
Lara Young (6)	182
Jessica Birch (6)	183
Otis Brett-Ferguson (5)	184

St Jude's CE Primary Academy, Wolverhampton

Khya Alarna Mal (5)	185

St Mary's CE Primary School, Credenhill

Teddy Bescoby (6)	186
Pippa Morgan (6)	187
Posie Taylor (5)	188
Leighton Holmes (6)	189
Elsie-Grace White (6)	190
Thea Lewis (5)	191
Nathan Thomson (6)	192
Kristian Miles (6)	193
Holly Adamson (6)	194
Sophie Adair (5)	195
Jacob Diaconu (6)	196
Lily Townley-Taylor (5)	197
Imogen French (6)	198
Ethan Clarke (5)	199
Tyler Jones (6), Alanah Thomas (6) & Evie	200
Lucas Privett (5)	201
Laci May Evans (6)	202
Michael Major (6)	203

The Kingsley School For Girls, Leamington Spa

Tabea Gwosdz (8)	204
Valentina Gwosdz (6)	205
Maelann Rodgers-Jourdenais (7)	206
Alex Thorp (5)	207
Kitty Sullivan (7)	208
Liana Hanson (7)	209
Juli Mueller-Piefkowski (7)	210
Lara Dolly Elliman (7)	211
Lydia de Cates (5)	212
Elia Iyieke (5)	213

Tiverton Junior & Infant School, Selly Oak

Zechariah McIlwain (6)	214
Dano Najmadeen A. Muhamad (6)	215
Lucas Stasiak (6)	216
Joycelyn Asare-Bediako (5)	217

The Poems

Delicious Pancake Bite

A pancake looks like a dreaming rat.
A pancake smells like a banana hat.
A pancake tastes like a marshmallow bite.
A pancake sounds like a happy flying kite.
A pancake feels like a soggy great fight.
A pancake disappears like a good idea in the middle of the night.

Riytal Khalid Abdulhamid Ali (6)
Al-Hijrah School, Bordesley Green

Rainbow

R ainbow, rainbow shock, wow!
A mazing colours
I n your rainbow
N ew colours are
B lue, green
O range is a rainbow colour
W here is the rainbow?

Hiba Noor (6)
Anderton Park Primary School, Sparkhill

Snow

S now is fun
N ow you can put on your hat, coat, scarf, gloves and boots.
O n the snow, you can play with snowflakes and build a snowman.
W indows are white when it snows.

Latifat Darasimi Onakoya (6)
Anderton Park Primary School, Sparkhill

Rainbow

R ainbow, rainbow, shocks me
A mazing colours
I n your rainbow
N ew colours
B lue, green, red, yellow colours
O n your rainbow
W indow.

Zakariyah Ibn Sheraz (5)
Anderton Park Primary School, Sparkhill

Sparkly Sun

S parkly sunshine, where's your yellow shiny colour?
U nder the bright sunshine you could go to the beach
N ow it's a sunny day, we will be sweaty.

Fatimah Ahmed (6)
Anderton Park Primary School, Sparkhill

Rain

R aindrops falling from the sky
A nd wind coming from the side
I t makes trees fall down
N ext, the cars can't go.

Dyam Yasin (6)
Anderton Park Primary School, Sparkhill

Snow

S nowflakes come from the sky
N o way, I never saw icicles
O h wow, icicles on the car
W arm clothes make you warm.

Kashan Ali (6)
Anderton Park Primary School, Sparkhill

Snow

S nowflakes falling down
N ever beneath your feet
O n the windows
W henever we play with snow.

Areeba Iqbal (6)
Anderton Park Primary School, Sparkhill

Sun

S hining in the sky
U nder the sea
N ever-ending on a hot day.

Amelia Uddin (5)
Anderton Park Primary School, Sparkhill

Raindrops

R unning water coming from grey clouds
A nd it's a very cold day
I need to put on my raincoat
N ow I'm ready to play
D ressed in wellies and a
R ainproof hat
O pening my umbrella, jumping in
P uddles, I make a...
S *plat!*

Lana Richards (7)
Anson CE Primary School, Great Haywood

Rabbit

R abbits I like
A round the field, they bounce
B ig, floppy ears
B ig, soft paws
I cy, blue eyes
T ickly tails.

Jessica Rose Mullins (7)
Anson CE Primary School, Great Haywood

Royal

I wear a crown
People bow to me
I sit on a throne
I am powerful
I have servants.
What am I?

Answer: A king.

Oscar Stevens (6)
Anson CE Primary School, Great Haywood

Ava Rose

A m I a girl? Yes I am and I work hard.
V ans are big, very big. Black and white are great.
A car is fast on the road, up and down they go.

R oses are red, very red. Pick them and smell.
O ctagons have got eight points and eight flat bits.
S o kind, I am. I help people when they fall over.
E very day I go for walks with my mum and dad.

Ava Rose Hayes (6)
Astley CE Primary School, Astley

Isabelle

I sabelle is the name my mum gave me
S ee, it really is
A lways helping others
B eautiful and helping
E veryone knows me
L earning is my favourite at school
L earning, I love so much
E very day is the best.

Isabelle Colgan (5)
Astley CE Primary School, Astley

Esme Ray

E sme is the name my mum gave me
S ometimes sad but mostly happy
M um loves me and my brother too
E veryone loves Esme

R ed is my favourite colour
A pples are red and juicy
Y ellow is a primary colour.

Esme Ray (6)
Astley CE Primary School, Astley

Cheetah

C heetahs are so very fast
H ave so much strength
E very day they zoom past
E ating like a tiger
T hey can climb higher
A wesome creatures
H abitats are the jungle.

Tyler Jones (6)
Astley CE Primary School, Astley

The Shark In The Sea

I can swim but I cannot go on Earth
I can jump and I make a big splash
I get humans and other fish
I can move my tail to swim
I have sharp teeth
I am a shark.

Naomi Harvey (6)
Astley CE Primary School, Astley

I Jump

I sound very quiet.
I am fluffy and soft and smooth and puffy.
I smell of dust.
I have small eyes.
My ears are long.
I have a small body.
My eyes are small.
I smell of hair.
You will find me under the trees.
What am I?

Zahrah Noor (5)
Blakesley Hall Primary School, Birmingham

My Animal Roar

I smell like a jungle.
I feel like a soft teddy.
My growl is as loud as a big crowd of people.
I look like an animal that has orange and black stripes.
I am always very hungry.
I eat little animals.
I chase people a lot.
I like to walk in the jungle.
What am I?

Sarah Shinvari (6)
Blakesley Hall Primary School, Birmingham

What Am I?

I am grey and tall.
I smell like hay.
My skin feels hard.
I sound loud and noisy.
I have big ears and a big, long nose.
What am I?

Mary Kamara (6)
Blakesley Hall Primary School, Birmingham

What Am I?

I have scaly skin.
I have a forked tongue.
I sound like a hissing sound.
I am very long.
My patterns are stripes.
What am I?

Jeniah Emanuel-Gardener (6)
Blakesley Hall Primary School, Birmingham

I Eat Hay

I smell like hay.
I feel like fluff.
I sound quiet.
My eyes are shiny.
You will find me with my mum.
I am little, like a mouse.
I eat hay.
I am really small.
I have tiny eyes.
I have two wings.
What am I?

Zoya Hussain
Blakesley Hall Primary School, Birmingham

Flopsy With Long Ears

I have big eyes and small feet.
I am smooth.
I am small and soft.
I feel happy.
I am as quiet as a mouse.
You will find me in a hole.
My claws are as sharp as scissors.
I am as black as a black cat.
What am I?

Tayyiba Gous (5)
Blakesley Hall Primary School, Birmingham

Let's Go Diving

I have people swimming in me.
On summer days, I'm perfect.
You can swim in me.
You can find me at the leisure centre.
I'm as deep as the ocean.
What am I?

Answer: A swimming pool.

Kawthar Nyanzi (6)
Blakesley Hall Primary School, Birmingham

The Green Scales

I feel scaly and spiky.
I smell smoky and leafy.
I sound extremely loud, as loud as a whale.
I look like burning hot fire.
I have a red and orange pattern on my body.
I have green scales.
What am I?

Mohammad Yousaf (6)
Blakesley Hall Primary School, Birmingham

Smooth Animal

I'm as smooth as a cheetah.
I smell of the salty sea.
I am as quiet as a mouse.
You will find me in the sea.
My eyes are as blue as the sky.
My tail is as strong as an elephant.
What am I?

Jarrai Drammeh (6)
Blakesley Hall Primary School, Birmingham

The Fire Animal

I sound like an elephant.
I fly very high.
I have big eyes that are as red as fire.
I feel hard like a rock.
On me, I have horns on the top of my head.
I live in a dark, big cave.
What am I?

Sania Shabraz (6)
Blakesley Hall Primary School, Birmingham

Carnivores

I have a long tail.
I have black stripes.
I like eating.
I am a meat-eater.
I sound like *roar!*
I'm as fast as a cheetah.
What am I?

Answer: A tiger.

Hasan Khan (6)
Blakesley Hall Primary School, Birmingham

Superhero

I have pink, straight, neat lines.
I have a hoodie.
I'm fast.
I can shoot webs out of my hands.
I crawl like a spider.
Who am I?

Answer: Spider-Gwen.

Inaaya Tariq (6)
Blakesley Hall Primary School, Birmingham

Speedy Animal

I have black eyes.
I am fast.
I am orange.
I have black spots.
I have sharp teeth.
I'm as fast as a lion.
What am I?

Answer: A cheetah.

Logan Quinn-Heffernan (6)
Blakesley Hall Primary School, Birmingham

Cute

I have four paws.
I have a long tail.
I like milk.
I am soft.
I'm as playful as a puppy.
I like to play.
What am I?

Answer: A cat

Khadija Naveed (6)
Blakesley Hall Primary School, Birmingham

Ice Friend

I have white fur.
I am as big as a tree.
I have a black nose.
I have two brown eyes.
I like to eat big fish or small fish.
My teeth are sharp.
What am I?

Aahadh Muhammed (6)
Blakesley Hall Primary School, Birmingham

My Best Friend

I have two legs.
I have a tail.
I like cuddles.
I am soft.
I am brown.
I'm as soft as a fox.
What am I?

Answer: My teddy bear.

Wali Mohammad Ghouri (6)
Blakesley Hall Primary School, Birmingham

Fish House

I have blue water.
I have deep water.
I am watery.
I have sharks and starfish.
I'm as wet as water.
What am I?

Answer: *The ocean.*

Rawdha Nyanzi (6)
Blakesley Hall Primary School, Birmingham

Carnivore

I have sharp teeth.
I have a tail.
I like meat.
I sound like *roar!*
I eat people's chickens.
What am I?

Answer: A lion.

Anisah Haseeb (5)
Blakesley Hall Primary School, Birmingham

What Am I?

I smell like a pack of hay.
I am ginormous and big and grey.
I am as tall as a tree.
I sound like a big roar.
I feel like a hard brick.
What am I?

Jennah Nawaz (5)
Blakesley Hall Primary School, Birmingham

My Furry Friend

I have white fur, like snow.
You will find me on the freezing ice.
I love raw fish.
I am as big as a house.
I am as furry as a cat.
What am I?

Darcie-Ann Evans (5)
Blakesley Hall Primary School, Birmingham

My Animal Roar

I am orange and black.
I am stripy.
I am like a cat.
My tail is as long as a shark.
I am soft and furry.
I growl and roar.
What am I?

Aleeza Yasin (6)
Blakesley Hall Primary School, Birmingham

What Am I?

I am grey and tall.
I smell like hay.
My skin feels hard.
I sound loud and noisy.
I have big ears and a long nose and fat legs.
What am I?

Abdullah Naveed (6) & Delia
Blakesley Hall Primary School, Birmingham

Bounce

I am smooth and soft and fluffy.
I can jump.
I have shiny eyes.
I have a pouch.
I have a small head.
I am quiet.
What am I?

Sabrene Messeded (6)
Blakesley Hall Primary School, Birmingham

Fast

I am orange and black and big.
I am soft and hard.
I live in the jungle.
I am scary.
I have sharp claws.
What am I?

Abigail Louise Smith (6)
Blakesley Hall Primary School, Birmingham

Cute

I have four paws.
I have two eyes.
I can scratch you.
I like to say meow.
What am I?

Answer: A cat.

Ethan Dolphin (6)
Blakesley Hall Primary School, Birmingham

Underwater Animal

I am silver.
My teeth are as sharp as claws.
I have a fin.
I am as tall as a house.
I have a sharp face
What am I?

Burhaan Nehman Haq (5)
Blakesley Hall Primary School, Birmingham

The Dusty Animal

I am as loud as a horn.
You will find me in Africa.
I have a trunk.
I am tall with four legs.
What am I?

Mohammad Azaan (5)
Blakesley Hall Primary School, Birmingham

Ocean Animal

I have a fin and a tail.
I am blue.
I swim in the pool.
What am I?

Answer: A dolphin.

Halimah Ali (5)
Blakesley Hall Primary School, Birmingham

Spring Is Here

Spring smells like beautiful roses.
Spring smells like sweet lavender.
Spring tastes like pumpkins.
Spring tastes like fruit that has been grown.
Spring sounds like raindrops dripping.
Spring sounds like people munching chocolate eggs.
Spring looks like a bird finding food for its family.
Spring looks like fish leaping out of the water.
Spring feels like a bird's light feathers.
Spring feels like silky grass.

Amia Gibson
Brownmead Primary Academy, Shard End

Summer

In summer, it's really hot because the sun is out and shining on me.
In summer, you need sun cream because it is very hot.
In summer, you need a hat because your head gets hot.
In summer, you need a swimming suit.
I can taste ice cream and smell beautiful flowers.
I can touch the water.
I can hear people screaming.

Leilah Khan (7)
Brownmead Primary Academy, Shard End

A Summer Poem

Summer is a beautiful season.
In summer, it's time to have a barbecue.
In summer, you have to put sun cream on.
In summer, you need to get the pool out.
In summer, all the flowers grow pretty.
Summer is a beautiful season.
Summer is a really hot season.
Summer is the best season.
In summer, you need lots of water.
In summer, stay in the garden all day.
In summer, you need ice in your water.
Summer is really hot... water balloons!

Ellie-May Ridings (7)
Brownmead Primary Academy, Shard End

The Mouse In The Kitchen

What was in the kitchen?
What could it be?
It was going *squeak, squeak!*
But still, what could it be?
I found a hole in my wall,
It was big, it was hairy,
It was a mouse!
Then it licked the cheese!

Macie Bayliss (7)
Brownmead Primary Academy, Shard End

Dinosaurs

D inosaurs are big, dinosaurs are small.
I saw one long ago.
N o one knows exactly what they look like,
O ther than me,
S o come and help me.
A fter, you can find out more about them.
U h no, dinosaurs are huge.
R un for your life from the terrifying T-rex.
S o come and help find some dinosaurs!

Serenity Ingram (7)
Brownmead Primary Academy, Shard End

Winter And Spring

Winter feels cold and icy.
In spring, it's a little bit cold.
Nicholas is Santa's name.
Robins as fluffy as snow.
Spring smells like chocolate eggs.
Spring is full of flowers.
Spring smells like fresh flowers.
Spring feels a little bit hot.
Winter feels super cold.
Winter tastes like a cold ice cream.

James Smith (7)
Brownmead Primary Academy, Shard End

Football

F ootball is a game, you can kick the ball.
O utside, I play football.
O utside, I play football all day.
T he football game was so good.
B ack at the football game.
A football game is so fun.
L ike that, I play every day.
L ove football all day.

Lucas Hewitt-Doyle (8)
Brownmead Primary Academy, Shard End

There's A Mouse In The Kitchen

M ouse in the kitchen eating last week's cheese.
O ddly eating birthday cake as well.
U nder the shed in the garden.
S queaking and shrieking.
E ating chips too.

Carter Fletcher (8)
Brownmead Primary Academy, Shard End

Dinosaurs

D inosaurs lived years ago.
I guanodon was a plant-eater.
N asty dinosaurs would bite you.
O h my goodness, a T-rex was big.
S tinky dino poop.
A llosaurus was a meat-eater.
U h oh, dinosaurs were big.
R unning away from predators.

Jack A P Murray (7)
Brownmead Primary Academy, Shard End

Winter

W hen it is cold, children play in the snow.
I n their houses, children have hot chocolate.
N o one put ice down people's backs!
T he children don't like the cold but they play in it.
E veryone's excited as Santa is
R iding on his sleigh.

Scarlett Coniff
Brownmead Primary Academy, Shard End

Winter

W inter smells like sweet buttercups.
I n winter, it looks like vanilla ice cream.
N ext, feed the multicoloured robin.
T each the robin to feed its babies.
E very day, feed the robins.
R obins are as soft as the snow.

Hollie Dowie (7)
Brownmead Primary Academy, Shard End

Fresh

What has a mouth that doesn't end?
What runs but doesn't have legs?
What has come from underground?
What is sky-blue like pretty bluebells?
What is as fresh as grass?
And what is as shiny as gold?
What is it?

Answer: A river.

Lamar Al-Karkhe (7)
Brownmead Primary Academy, Shard End

My Friend's Birthday Party

My friend invited me to his birthday party
We went outside to play a game, it felt warm.
We put the birthday hats on our heads.
We had delicious pudding, it tasted like flowers.
We went on the bouncy castle.
I jumped so high, I nearly touched the sky.

Caden Summers (6)
Brownmead Primary Academy, Shard End

Winter

W inter is very cold.
I n winter, it snows.
N ight-time in winter is dark and scary.
T hings in winter are covered in snowstorms.
E arwigs are cold in winter.
R aining snow is like hail.

Malik Elshazly (7)
Brownmead Primary Academy, Shard End

Spring

S pring is full of pretty flowers.
P ink and purple and red.
R oses bloom in springtime.
I n spring, it's sunny.
N ice in spring to go outside.
G o on a holiday in spring.

Reyhan Mohammed (7)
Brownmead Primary Academy, Shard End

Rugby

S port is hard, really hard.
P ut your arm up when you kick a rugby ball.
O n the way to tag you.
R un straight with the ball, not around.
T o avoid being tagged, trick them.

Ethan McAleenan (7)
Brownmead Primary Academy, Shard End

Winter

W inter is cold.
I t brings snow on our noses.
N o one is hot.
T he grass is covered with snow.
E veryone is excited about Santa,
R iding his sleigh.

Kiasha Delarami (7)
Brownmead Primary Academy, Shard End

Summer

Summer smells like flowers,
Summer sounds like birds tweeting,
Summer looks like ice cream melting,
Summer feels like a holiday,
Summer tastes like ice cream.

Orson Dell
Brownmead Primary Academy, Shard End

Spring

Spring smells like sweet flowers,
Spring feels warm,
Spring looks like a word,
Spring is full of flowers,
Spring tastes like hot cross buns.

Shareef Ibn Abdul-Kareem (7)
Brownmead Primary Academy, Shard End

My Dragon

My dragon tastes like chocolate
My dragon tastes like Coke.
My dragon tastes like sweet candy.
My dragon is like a soft teddy bear.
My dragon is kind.
My dragon is nice.
I like my dragon.
I love my dragon.
I like my dragon so much
And my dragon loves me.

Lawi Mohamed (6)
Chilwell Croft Academy, Birmingham

My Dragon

My dragon feels soft.
My dragon smells like perfume.
My dragon sounds like a normal voice.
My dragon tastes like white chocolate cake.
I love my dragon.

Rabia Mahamed (6)
Chilwell Croft Academy, Birmingham

My Dragon

My dragon looks like a flyer.
My dragon feels like the best king in the world.
My dragon smells like pizza.
My dragon sounds like a robot.
I love my dragon.

Rami Bashir (6)
Chilwell Croft Academy, Birmingham

Tell Me A Dragon

My dragon is a gold dragon and it's got emerald eyes.
My dragon looks like gold and a big school.
My dragon sounds like butterflies.
My dragon feels like a teddy bear.
My dragon tastes like candy.
I love my dragon!

Abdullah Mohammad Abdallah (5)
Chilwell Croft Academy, Birmingham

My Dragon

My dragon looks like a light star.
My dragon feels like a fluffy cushion.
My dragon smells like strawberry cake.
My dragon sounds like a scary lion roaring.
My dragon tastes like a chilli pepper.
I love my dragon.

Aisha Abdihalim Ahmed (6)
Chilwell Croft Academy, Birmingham

My Dragon

My dragon looks like a unicorn.
My dragon feels like a soft cushion.
My dragon smells like chocolate.
My dragon sounds like beautiful girls singing.
My dragon tastes like bubblegum.
I love my dragon.

Caia Patterson (6)
Chilwell Croft Academy, Birmingham

My Dragon

My dragon looks like a special and cool dragon.
My dragon feels like a soft cushion.
My dragon smells like chocolate.
My dragon sounds like a sweet dragon.
My dragon tastes like a white chocolate bar.

Elham Alhassan Safianu (6)
Chilwell Croft Academy, Birmingham

My Dragon

My dragon is a unicorn dragon and he has a nose with two big holes.
My dragon looks like a princess.
My dragon sounds like a racing car.
My dragon tastes like bubblegum.
I love my best dragon.

Hafiza Begum (6)
Chilwell Croft Academy, Birmingham

My Dragon

My dragon looks like chocolate cake.
My dragon sounds like music.
My dragon smells like perfume.
My dragon feels soft.
My dragon tastes like chicken.
I love my dragon.

Abdulrahman Musse (6)
Chilwell Croft Academy, Birmingham

My Dragon

My dragon looks like a unicorn,
My dragon sounds like a snoring man,
My dragon smells like strawberries.

Anaya Uddin (6)
Chilwell Croft Academy, Birmingham

My Dragon

My dragon looks like a sausage.
My dragon smells like a cat.
If feels like a soft cushion.

Mikail Thomas (6)
Chilwell Croft Academy, Birmingham

My Dragon

My dragon looks like mud.
My dragon feels like a smooth mat.
My dragon smells like fire.

Junior Kisibu Kimuolo (6)
Chilwell Croft Academy, Birmingham

Bunny

B ouncing in a meadow
U nder the warm ground, he lives
N ibbling his tasty food
N ice and soft fur
Y oung, fluffy baby

R unning around with his sisters
A lert to danger
B urrowing underground
B iting crunchy grass
I nto the earth, he lies
T ime to sleep in his bed.

Phoebe King (7)
Earlsdon Primary School, Coventry

All About Things And Animals

Yesterday, I saw a dog in a bog
I saw a hog with a dog
And I saw a cat on a mat with a hat
I saw a mouse chasing a louse
And ran into its house
I saw a deer with one big ear
Who was full of fear
I saw a pig hug a jug
I saw a mole that made a hole
And he hurt my soul
I saw a bunny eat honey
And it was very funny.

Dolly May Wignall (7)
Earlsdon Primary School, Coventry

A Little Bird

A little bird called Jack
Heard a big, loud crack
He was scared and surprised
Couldn't move, terrified
He was hiding in his nest
And was having a rest
Jack woke up, screaming
All along he'd been dreaming
He spent 10,000 quid
For a squid
He spent 800 pounds
On some clowns.

William Senaux (6)
Earlsdon Primary School, Coventry

Summery Times

Summer is a great sunny time
It's lovely, especially the beach
When you have ice cream and summery stuff
Like shorts and bare feet on the beach
Sun in the sky and kites flying high
Sunglasses and fun with family and friends
Butterflies flying around and singing birds.
Hope you have a great time!

Rand Alyasin (6)
Earlsdon Primary School, Coventry

Holidays

H appy children go to the beach
O cean creatures to be found
L ate nights playing games
I ce creams in the sun
D ancing around the campfire
A dventures every day
Y achts bobbing on the sea
S un shining around.

Oliver (7)
Earlsdon Primary School, Coventry

A Holiday That I Have Been On

D eckchairs on the gold sand
O cean sparkles in the sunshine
R ed squirrels on a brown sea island
S eagulls diving for our fish and chips
E xciting families on the beach
T iny crabs in the rock pools.

Eliza Slack (7)
Earlsdon Primary School, Coventry

Singing

S ounds really fun
I magine it in your head
N ice things you would hear
G reat feeling in your heart
I t's exciting in my ears!
N ever stop singing
G ood things happen when you sing.

Hazel Fawcett (6)
Earlsdon Primary School, Coventry

What Am I?

I am a glamorous, magical animal
I have a gold, shimmering, shiny horn
I have a pink fluffy mane and also have a pink fluffy tail
I have snowy wings
What am I?

Answer: A unicorn.

Alayna Quayum (6)
Earlsdon Primary School, Coventry

What Am I...?

I go under bridges, but not over
I have lots of rubbish but I'm nice to jump in
I run through London but I have no legs.
What am I?

Answer: *The River Thames.*

Tom Smith (6)
Earlsdon Primary School, Coventry

Summer!

Summer is hot, like the scorching sun
Summer grows flowers
Summer, some grass grows
Summer, the sun comes out
Summer is fun
Summer, you need to wear a hat.

Dora Wang (6)
Earlsdon Primary School, Coventry

The Beautiful Star

S hining bright
T winkling at night
A lways there
R ewrite the stars
S un comes out and then goes back in.

Almaya Lily Carrott (6)
Earlsdon Primary School, Coventry

Great Fire

G reat fire
R ough flames
E ngulfing flames
A nxious people
T he houses, blockbusters and explosions

F lashing lights
I n the houses
R ed arches of light all over the place
E xplosions everywhere.

Lorenzo Tushe (7)
Hanley St Luke's CE (A) Primary School, Hanley

Snow

S nowflakes are frosty and white
N ice, white snowflakes, frosty cold
O h, it's frosty, there is snow
W hen it falls onto the ground, you don't know which ones are which.

Sama Sultani (7)
Hanley St Luke's CE (A) Primary School, Hanley

Planet

P is for planets.
L is for light from the sun.
A is for astronauts in a rocket.
N is for Neptune, big and round.
E is for Earth.
T is for taking a rocket to space.

Ayanna Mambiri
Harper Bell SDA School, Birmingham

Space

S pace is where you find lots of planets.
P ut on the spacesuit.
A stronauts go in a rocket.
C omets are made of rocks.
E arth is where we live.

Jada Johnson (5)
Harper Bell SDA School, Birmingham

Earth

E arth is in space.
A n ant is on my foot.
R ockets go from Earth to space.
T omorrow is a happy day.
H ow will you play with me?

Nasir Muhammad (5)
Harper Bell SDA School, Birmingham

Astronaut

S paceships land on the moon.
P lanets go around the sun.
A stronauts floating in the rocket.
C an you see the sun,
E veryone?

Marcel Baker (5)
Harper Bell SDA School, Birmingham

Space

S un is burning.
P luto is tiny.
A stronauts go to space in a rocket.
C omet flies to space.
E arth is where we live.

Ruel Worrell (5)
Harper Bell SDA School, Birmingham

Sun

S is for the hot sun.
P is for the planets.
A is for astronauts.
C is for comets.
E is for Earth.

Ashantae Samuels (5)
Harper Bell SDA School, Birmingham

The Moon

M atthew loves the moon.
O n the moon, it's empty.
O n the moon, it is cold.
N ight-time, the moon goes down.

Matthew Deen-Piper (4)
Harper Bell SDA School, Birmingham

The Sun

S un, it makes everything bright.
U nder the sun, it is hot.
N ight-time, I go to bed and the sun goes down.

Alayah Ward (5)
Harper Bell SDA School, Birmingham

The Sun

S un is shining in the day.
U niverse has a gigantic hot sun.
N ight is when the sun goes down.

Semi Awoniranye (5)
Harper Bell SDA School, Birmingham

Space

S un, it is a big round circle.
U niverse has nine planets.
N ight is when the moon comes out.

Esther Nealson (5)
Harper Bell SDA School, Birmingham

Sun

S un, it is hot like lava.
U p in the sky, big and round.
N ight-time, the sun is not bright.

Tasia-Ray Berryman (5)
Harper Bell SDA School, Birmingham

Fire

S un has heat and fire.
U p in the sky, burning bright.
N ight makes the sun go down.

Jordan Kerr (5)
Harper Bell SDA School, Birmingham

The Sun

S un, it is hot.
U nder the moon, it's bright.
N ight is when the sun goes down.

Cienna Thomas (4)
Harper Bell SDA School, Birmingham

Space Food

F is for fig.
O is for orange.
O is for onions.
D is for dinnertime.

Daniella Deen-Piper (4)
Harper Bell SDA School, Birmingham

Sun

S un, it is a bright star.
U p in the shiny sky.
N o sun in the sky at night.

Fatima (5)
Harper Bell SDA School, Birmingham

Who Am I?

I wear pink lipstick and wear red nail polish
For meals, I wear my best clothes for the queen and king to see
And I sit on the throne that is golden
I love golden jewels
I have a golden bracelet, golden necklace and golden rings
What am I?

Answer: A princess.

Alicia Berrow (5)
Nathaniel Newton Infant School, Hartshill

What Am I?

I have a beautiful dress and it is blue and I live in a castle
I am a girl
I wear jewellery
My mum is the queen
And my dad is the king
I have cute hair and it is gold
I have a frilly dress.
What am I?

Answer: A princess.

Macie Moss (6)
Nathaniel Newton Infant School, Hartshill

What Am I?

I am good at fighting dragons
I have a sword
I am good at fighting bad guys
You might see me hiding from dragons
I live in a castle
I wear a suit of armour.
What am I?

Answer: A knight.

Joseph Dawson (6)
Nathaniel Newton Infant School, Hartshill

What Am I?

I have short legs
You might see me in a cave
I am red
I breathe fire
I have scaly skin
I have big, pointy ears
I am dangerous
I have sharp claws.
What am I?

Answer: A dragon.

Indy Burbury (6)
Nathaniel Newton Infant School, Hartshill

What Am I?

I have long towers, battlements and a moat
I have grey walls and arrow loops in the wall
I have small windows and a throne
I have a big, long drawbridge.
What am I?

Answer: A castle.

Aaron Gabriel Szanto (6)
Nathaniel Newton Infant School, Hartshill

What Am I?

I frighten my opponents when I am in a battle
My dragon is green and it has orange eyes
And my dragon can breathe fire
The fire is orange and bright red.
What am I?

Answer: A knight.

Archie Brown (6)
Nathaniel Newton Infant School, Hartshill

What Am I?

I am very, very brave
I have big wings
I am good at breathing fire
You might see me flying through the night
I live in a cave
I breathe fire
What am I?

Answer: A dragon.

Archie Jennings (6)
Nathaniel Newton Infant School, Hartshill

What Am I?

I am brave
I have a sword
I am good at using a sword
You might see me riding a horse
I live in a grey castle
I wear silver, metal clothes.
What am I?

Answer: A knight.

Harry Dunbar (5)
Nathaniel Newton Infant School, Hartshill

What Am I?

I am beautiful
I have a crown
I am good at doing my chores
You might see me at the castle
I live in a palace
I am in a beautiful dress.
What am I?

Answer: A princess.

Ellie Gabrielle Malkin (6)
Nathaniel Newton Infant School, Hartshill

What Am I?

You might see me by a castle
I am very, very strong
I have a sword and shield
I am good at fighting
I live in a castle
I fight dragons.
What am I?

Answer: A knight.

Callum Cullen (6)
Nathaniel Newton Infant School, Hartshill

What Am I?

I am orange and I breathe fire
I am green and frightening
I can blow a loud roar
I stomp and fight knights
I am fighting to look for food.
What am I?

Answer: A dragon.

Archie Hargreaves (6)
Nathaniel Newton Infant School, Hartshill

What Am I?

I am so very brave
I have a scaly body
I am good at breathing fire
You might see me flying
I live in a cave
I have a squishy tail
What am I?

Answer: A dragon.

Jackson Dudley (6)
Nathaniel Newton Infant School, Hartshill

What Am I?

I am brave
I have scaly skin
I am good at breathing fire
You might see me in a cave
I live in a cave
I always go to fight knights
What am I?

Answer: A dragon.

Saiya Patel (6)
Nathaniel Newton Infant School, Hartshill

What Am I?

I am really strong
I have turrets
I am good at staying still
You might see me staying there
I live in a field
I have arrow slots.
What am I?

Answer: A castle.

George Thomas Weaver (6)
Nathaniel Newton Infant School, Hartshill

What Am I?

I am very brave
I have a sword
I am good at fighting
You might see me at war
I live in a castle
I shoot with my bow and arrow.
What am I?

Answer: A knight.

Bentley Smalley (6)
Nathaniel Newton Infant School, Hartshill

What Am I?

I am very brave
I have sharp claws
I am good at breathing fire
You might see me in a cave
I live in a cave
I am very big.
What am I?

Answer: A dragon.

Stanley Deuster (6)
Nathaniel Newton Infant School, Hartshill

What Am I?

I am very brave
I have metal boots
I am good at fighting
You might see me saving a princess
I live in a castle
I fight.
What am I?

Answer: A knight.

Jack Dani Luke Flannery (5)
Nathaniel Newton Infant School, Hartshill

What Am I?

I am yellow and silver and attack people in battle
I am powerful, sharp and long
A knight holds me like a weapon
I am a weapon.
What am I?

Answer: A sword.

Jaden Charters (6)
Nathaniel Newton Infant School, Hartshill

What Am I?

I have a golden tiara on my head
I am helpful to the king and queen
I call them Mum and Dad
I'm waiting for my prince.
What am I?

Answer: A princess.

Khloé Mullis (5)
Nathaniel Newton Infant School, Hartshill

What Am I?

I'm beautiful and caring
I'm scared of dragons
I wear a shiny tiara
My mum is the queen
My dad is the king.
What am I?

Answer: A princess.

Harry Robert Wright (6)
Nathaniel Newton Infant School, Hartshill

What Am I?

I breathe out fire when I see you
I am deadly and aggressive
I am enormous and have pointy teeth
My wings beat like a drum
What am I?

Answer: A dragon.

David Lukash-Alexeenko (6)
Nathaniel Newton Infant School, Hartshill

What Am I?

I have pointy teeth
I'm strong and deadly
My scales shine in the sun
I am bloody
I breathe smoke as I breathe.
What am I?

Answer: A dragon.

Georgina Whale (6)
Nathaniel Newton Infant School, Hartshill

What Am I?

I can fly
I am purple with black dots
I can breathe fire
The knight caught me in the castle
He put me in prison
What am I?

Answer: A dragon.

Charlie Bliss (6)
Nathaniel Newton Infant School, Hartshill

What Am I?

I am blue
I have wings
I am good at surfing
You might see me in the sky
I live in a cave
I breathe fire.
What am I?

Answer: A dragon.

Carly Underwood (6)
Nathaniel Newton Infant School, Hartshill

What Am I?

I am a knight's best friend
I am pointy and sharp
I am strong and I guard
A knight throws me
I protect him
What am I?

Answer: A spear.

George Dyde (6)
Nathaniel Newton Infant School, Hartshill

What Am I?

I am dark
It is cold and very quiet
There is no escape
It is very scary
I am beneath the castle floor
What am I?

Answer: A dragon.

Shannon Bullock (6)
Nathaniel Newton Infant School, Hartshill

What Am I?

I am creaky
I am not straight
I have handles
You go up and down me
I spin round and round.
What am I?

Answer: A spiral staircase.

Millie Johnston (6)
Nathaniel Newton Infant School, Hartshill

What Am I?

I am a knight's best friend
I protect his body
If you hit me, I won't die
I'm made of metal.
What am I?

Answer: A shield.

Harshaan Singh Gill (6)
Nathaniel Newton Infant School, Hartshill

What Am I?

I am strong
Don't fight me
I wear chainmail
I look through a visor
And carry a shield.
What am I?

Answer: A knight.

Nedas Jonikas (6)
Nathaniel Newton Infant School, Hartshill

What Am I?

I have green, shiny scales
I have sharp teeth
I am strong
My wings flap like a bird.
What am I?

Answer: A dragon.

Kai Piff (6)
Nathaniel Newton Infant School, Hartshill

What Am I?

I have sharp teeth and a scaly back
I am vicious
I have sharp teeth
I breathe fire.
What am I?

Answer: A dragon.

Layla Rose Yates (6)
Nathaniel Newton Infant School, Hartshill

What Am I?

I am fierce and scary
I breathe out fire
I fly across the sky
My teeth are sharp.
What am I?

Answer: A dragon.

Juan Martinez (6)
Nathaniel Newton Infant School, Hartshill

What Am I?

I go around and around
I spin up and down
I go creak when you step on me.
What am I?

Answer: A spiral staircase.

Marnie Hughes (6)
Nathaniel Newton Infant School, Hartshill

What Am I?

I am bright, shiny silver
I am made of metal
I can chop the enemies' heads off.
What am I?

Answer: A sword.

Hadley Hemmings (6)
Nathaniel Newton Infant School, Hartshill

What Am I?

I am silver and I can kill enemies
And a knight holds me
I am sharp and powerful
What am I?

Answer: A sword.

Luke Britton (5)
Nathaniel Newton Infant School, Hartshill

What Am I?

I am brave and strong
I have a sword
I ride a horse
I wear silver armour.
What am I?

Answer: A knight.

Steven-Junior Bliss (6)
Nathaniel Newton Infant School, Hartshill

What Am I?

I breathe fire
I am green and scaly
My teeth are sharp and frightening.
What am I?

Answer: A dragon.

Annabelle Wood (7)
Nathaniel Newton Infant School, Hartshill

What Am I?

I am a girl
I live in the castle
I know a dragon with a beautiful white tummy.
What am I?

Answer: A princess.

Alfie Wayne Austin (6)
Nathaniel Newton Infant School, Hartshill

What Am I?

I creak
I go up and down
I spin around
I am wooden.
What am I?

Answer: A spiral staircase.

Hollie May Gibson (6)
Nathaniel Newton Infant School, Hartshill

What Am I?

I have a sharp sword
I protect the king in battle
I am strong.
What am I?

Answer: A knight.

Corey Malyon (6)
Nathaniel Newton Infant School, Hartshill

What Am I?

I breathe out fire
I am vicious and have a tail
My wings flap.
What am I?

Answer: A dragon. (upside down)

Keira White (5)
Nathaniel Newton Infant School, Hartshill

What Am I?

I am red
I breathe fire
My wings are big
I kill knights.
What am I?

Answer: A dragon.

Maisie-Lynne Franklin (6)
Nathaniel Newton Infant School, Hartshill

What Am I?

I am pointy and sparkly
I am shiny
You can find me in a crown.
What am I?

Answer: A jewel.

Ralph Oliver Baker (6)
Nathaniel Newton Infant School, Hartshill

What Am I?

I am green
I have got scaly skin
I am gigantic and I am red.
What am I?

Answer: A dragon.

Jack Maxie Dodds (6)
Nathaniel Newton Infant School, Hartshill

What Am I?

I am green
I am fierce
I can fly
I breathe fire.
What am I?

Answer: A dragon.

Oliver Astley (6)
Nathaniel Newton Infant School, Hartshill

What Am I?

I fight dragons
I wear a helmet
I have a sword.
What am I?

Answer: A knight.

Lewis Stevens (6)
Nathaniel Newton Infant School, Hartshill

What Am I?

I can breathe fire
I can fight
I can fly high.
What am I?

Answer: A dragon.

Ruben Darlison (5)
Nathaniel Newton Infant School, Hartshill

What Am I?

I have a sword
I wear a helmet
I fight people
What am I?

Answer: A knight.

Logan Vaughan Bound (6)
Nathaniel Newton Infant School, Hartshill

Fit, Not Fat

Big balls, small balls or no balls at all.
Sometimes outside or perhaps in a hall.
I use energy and muscles from all over my body.
I need goals, rackets or the floor depending on what I do.
Sometimes on your own or sometimes in a team.
I can be a hobby, just for fun or I can be a full-time job.
What am I?

Answer: Sport.

Georgia Smith (7)
Nelson Primary School, Birmingham

The King Who Likes Having Fun And Eating

I am the king of goodness,
Although I am a king,
I never hurt people,
Because I like to have fun,
It keeps me happy,
I can laugh until I can't stop,
As I love to eat more,
I get more food,
Exhausted, I will vomit,
I sit back and relax on my fluffy chair,
Beneath my castle,
And recover from my belly,
It takes me one hour and thirty minutes,
My guards are quite happy,
My food is clean, take a piece,
While I have fun,

I sit,
For the next thirty minutes,
And eat the pieces,
Now, when I've finished,
I go to the ocean,
And wash my hands,
They're very clean,
It's very easy,
Because my castle is near,
I'm happy to be a king.

Ankhang Nguyen (7)
Nelson Primary School, Birmingham

Winter

I come in winter, in December, when people sleep or maybe not.
I have a red coat and a black belt and black boots.
I have magical pet reindeer and a fluffy, white and soft beard.
I have a flying sleigh and I'm the opposite of the Grinch.
Who am I?

Answer: Santa Claus.

Mohtady Bashir (7)
Nelson Primary School, Birmingham

Stripy Horse

She has golden wings,
You like it when she sings.
Her rainbow horn shines,
When this stripy horse dines.
She can make flowers,
With her magic powers.
Who is she?

Answer: A unicorn.

Lilja Teern (6)
Nelson Primary School, Birmingham

All About Me

K ind to everyone.
A lways ready to learn.
N ephew to aunts and uncles.
Y oung and free.
O nly son to my mummy
N icest boy you will ever meet.

Kanyon Armstrong (6)
Nelson Primary School, Birmingham

Tig And Tag

Tig and tag is so much fun,
I can play it all day long,
With your friends, if you're it,
You must run fast and far from the tagger.
If you're caught, then you are it.

Rayyan Ahmed (6)
Nelson Primary School, Birmingham

Fairy Land

F airies are magical creatures
A s they fly around your garden
I n and out of the flowers, they go
R ound and round the patio
Y ou can try to catch one but you never will

L ots of fairies live in your garden
A rriving every spring
N ectar gives them food to eat
D ancing is what keeps them on their feet.

Constance Harper Denton (6)
Our Lady & St Oswald's Catholic Primary School, Oswestry

My Bicycle

B icycles, bicycle, cycle as fast as you can
I can't believe I am going so fast
C ycling is hard to do but it is easy for you
Y ou are great at cycling, like me
C ycle like you are in a triathlon
L et's cycle around the lake today
E very time I cycle, I have lots of fun.

Alexandra Ali (6)
Our Lady & St Oswald's Catholic Primary School, Oswestry

My Holiday

H olding beautiful, pretty shells
O h, how the salty, blue sea smells
L icking lovely lollipops
I want an ice cream from that shop
D igging Devon's deep, soft sand
A ll this treasure in my hand
Y ay for holidays, surf and sun, lots of fun for everyone.

Herbie Brook Jones (6)
Our Lady & St Oswald's Catholic Primary School, Oswestry

A Trip To The Seaside

S urfing through the big waves
E ating yummy ice cream chocolate is the best
A crab scuttles by
S earching through the rockpools, guess what I can find?
I love building sandcastles
D iving through the waving sea
E njoying the summer sun.

Isabella Bentley (6)
Our Lady & St Oswald's Catholic Primary School, Oswestry

Sights And Sounds At The Seaside

I can taste the chocolate ice cream
I can feel the salty air in my mouth
I can smell the chips in the air
I can hear the waves crashing on the rocks
I can see the crabs and shells on the sand
I can see the sea coming in and out
I can go home when the sun goes down.

Arrabella Lucia Judd (6)
Our Lady & St Oswald's Catholic Primary School, Oswestry

Laughing At The Circus

L ittle people smiling, having wriggly, tickly fun
A t the circus watching silly clowns
U ncles and aunties joining in with the smiles
G iggling at the splatting custard pies
H appy laughing people in the giant, big top.

Lottie Grayston (6)
Our Lady & St Oswald's Catholic Primary School, Oswestry

It Hurts Creatures

My long waves
Crash upon rocks
My peaceful waters
Crawl upon the sand
The creatures of the land are happy
But my creatures aren't
Stop littering
And save the creatures
What am I?

Answer: *The sea.*

Ethan Jeremy Chavez (5)
Our Lady & St Oswald's Catholic Primary School, Oswestry

Seaside

S hiny sun
E verybody having fun
A mazing ice cream is really cold
S and is getting very soggy
I have some salty chips with some sauce
D ying fish in the sea
E xcellent sand making.

Kieron George Rhodes Chander Owen (7)
Our Lady & St Oswald's Catholic Primary School, Oswestry

A Special Person

I like to wear a big fluffy gown
I have an important job all year round
I like to be warm and love the sun
I have superpowers
I drive a shiny, white car
And have big golden hair
Who am I?

Answer: Mum.

Buddy Thomas (6)
Our Lady & St Oswald's Catholic Primary School, Oswestry

Space

S pace aliens, zooming through space
P eople blasting off 3, 2, 1
A stronauts walking on the moon
C osmic Milky Way sparkling in the sky
E arth spinning round and round.

William Abercrombie (7)
Our Lady & St Oswald's Catholic Primary School, Oswestry

What Dinosaur Am I?

I have spikes on my bendy armour
I am a herbivore
I eat plants with my tiny teeth
I defend myself with my clubbed tail
I've lived in the Cretaceous times.
What dinosaur am I?

Answer: Ankylosaurus.

Freddie Holdcroft (6)
Perry Hall Primary School, Wednesfield

Bunny Hops!

B unnies bouncing up and down
U p in the sky, in trees up high
N uts, it chews all day long
N aughty bunny stole the carrots
Y ummy, nommy carrots

R ain, rain, go away, come back another day
A corns drop, acorns please drop
B ig bunnies jumping up and down
B unny hopping, bunny hopping
I just wanna go eat my carrots
T ime to bounce.

Bella Gooding (5)
Rushall Primary School, Rushall

My Day At The Black Country Museum

At first we went back in time and discovered a coal mine.
The coal mine was cold, dark and damp, and to see we had to use a flash lamp.
A man took us on a tour of the mine underground, it was a little bit creepy and we couldn't hear a sound.

Our next stop was via the fish and chip shop, with plenty of salt and vinegar.
Then it was off to catch a film at the old-fashioned cinema.
The film we watched was in black and white and didn't have any sound.
Mom said because I was so good our next stop would be the fairground.

The fairground looked like lots of fun and I couldn't wait to try out a ride.
My favourite was the tall helter-skelter slide.
We had to sit on a straw mat and we slid round and round super fast.

Lastly, we caught an old fashioned bus back to the start.
Before they had buses, people would have travelled by horse and cart.
I had great fun learning about how we used to live in the olden days.
I'm just glad that our toilets have improved in so many ways!

Fletcher Christopher Kendrick (5)
Rushall Primary School, Rushall

Who Am I?

I'm muscly and red with a glowing heart
Bad guys best watch out before I shoot fire out my palms!
I have a hobby which I really enjoy
Where I collect art
Some people don't trust me
But I don't care
I'm here to serve this country
I'm not scared.
Who am I?

Answer: Iron Man.

Mason Smith (6)
Rushall Primary School, Rushall

A Magical Hero

I always wear round, black glasses
I have a lightning bolt scar on my forehead
My best friends are Ron and Hermione
I got to Hogwarts school
My house is Gryffindor
And I am the fastest Quidditch Seeker.
Who am I?

Answer: Harry Potter.

Mia Stephenson (6)
Rushall Primary School, Rushall

School Is Cool

My school is really cool
We need to be able to read
To plant a seed to help learn
Lunchtime is munch time
Full of laughs and now I'm ready for maths.

Wyatt Smith (5)
Rushall Primary School, Rushall

The Pets Poem

D ogs like balls
O ver in the park, we play
G olden doodle is one of my dogs
S ocks are my dog's favourite thing.

Jayden Austin (6)
Rushall Primary School, Rushall

Native American Ladies

Ladies are in charge
They tell the men what to hunt
For the food
They meet and use the skins for their clothes
And teepees.

Rosie-Mae (7)
Rushall Primary School, Rushall

Superheroes

S inister villains are destroying the world.
U nfortunately for them, heroes are in town!
P owers to save the day.
E veryone is very happy that the city is saved.
R escued citizens thank the heroes for their bravery.
"H elp!" a voice is screaming from a tall building
"E mergency!" a hero says.
R adical villains have imprisoned a citizen but the heroes help.
O range fireworks light up the sky and the town is peaceful.

Maximilian Schielke (7)
St Catherine Of Siena RC Primary School, Lee Bank

Trickery Time

I like to trick people when they read,
I am very tricky indeed!
High or low,
You try to solve me but never say no.
I have a question and an answer,
I am as hard as a thousand dancers,
And I am not a thing.
What am I?

Answer: A riddle.

Abigail Amanuel (7)
St Catherine Of Siena RC Primary School, Lee Bank

All About Chocolate

C hocolate is white, brown or dark.
H ave it at home, at the beach or at the park.
O nce you taste it, you can't stop.
C hocolate is sweet and yummy, hooray!
O nly a little, your teeth can decay.
L isten to music while it melts in your mouth
A nd sing and dance all around.
T ake a bite, just a little bit.
E verybody loves it!

Eduardo Banito (6)
St Edward's Catholic Primary School, Selly Park

Holiday

The soft sand is on my toes,
I can smell the sea in my nose.
I'm eating a yummy strawberry ice cream,
The sea is so green and blue that it gleams.
I'm looking forward to fish and chips,
And maybe some tomato sauce as a dip.
Up in the sky, I see the sun,
This is why holidays are so much fun.

Lara Young (6)
St Edward's Catholic Primary School, Selly Park

Sweets

S weets are not messy.
W hen it's summer, we can have vegetables and vegetables are healthy.
E veryone needs to be healthy,
E ven if they love sweets.
T imes like after reading, we can have sweets.
S ometimes we are allowed to eat sweets.

Jessica Birch (6)
St Edward's Catholic Primary School, Selly Park

Chickens

Chickens in the wild,
What a wonderful thing.
It is so nice to see a chicken being free
And it will lay a tasty egg for me.

Otis Brett-Ferguson (5)
St Edward's Catholic Primary School, Selly Park

My Brother, Che

Che is my brother, he is the best
I love him every day
He makes me feel blessed
We love to giggle and jiggle
Then we love to rest
My brother makes me happy
My mommy and daddy say
We are the *best!*

Khya Alarna Mal (5)
St Jude's CE Primary Academy, Wolverhampton

Summer

S ummer is fun
U nder the hot, yellow sun
M y mum is cooking for my family
M um is making dinner for me
E veryone is loving the dinner
R unning is fun.

Teddy Bescoby (6)
St Mary's CE Primary School, Credenhill

I Love Summer

S ummer is exciting
U nder the warm, yellow sun
M aking sandcastles at the beach
M um is making cupcakes
E veryone is happy
R iding my bike.

Pippa Morgan (6)
St Mary's CE Primary School, Credenhill

I Love Summer

S ummer is fun
U nder the shade
M y family are having fun
M aking pizzas
E ven Mum's busy blowing up the pool
R iding my bike every day.

Posie Taylor (5)
St Mary's CE Primary School, Credenhill

Summer

S ummer is fun
U nder the warm sun
M e and my dad ride our bikes
M aking Lego with Mum
E very day I go to the pool
R elaxing on the beach.

Leighton Holmes (6)
St Mary's CE Primary School, Credenhill

I Love Summer

S ummer is fun
U nder the water
M ummy is blowing up the swimming pool
M oney is everywhere
E veryone is happy
R un with my mum and dad.

Elsie-Grace White (6)
St Mary's CE Primary School, Credenhill

Summer

S ummer is fun
U nder the warm, yellow sun
M um is laughing
M um is making me a cake
E veryone is happy
R unning on the beach.

Thea Lewis (5)
St Mary's CE Primary School, Credenhill

Summer

S ummer is fun
U nder the hot, yellow sun
M aking sandcastles
M um is sitting in a chair
E veryone is happy
R unning around.

Nathan Thomson (6)
St Mary's CE Primary School, Credenhill

I Love Summer

S ummer is fun
U nder the warm sun
M um is making me laugh
M um is funny
E veryone is happy
R unning is fun.

Kristian Miles (6)
St Mary's CE Primary School, Credenhill

Sand

S ummer is playing
A round the swimming pool
N ow we can have a cold ice cream
D ancing on the golden sand.

Holly Adamson (6)
St Mary's CE Primary School, Credenhill

Summer

S ummer is beautiful
A round the swimming pool
N ow we can have a cold ice cream
D o you feel happy?

Sophie Adair (5)
St Mary's CE Primary School, Credenhill

Sand

S unny days
A round the swimming pool
N ow we can have a cold ice cream
D ancing on the golden sand.

Jacob Diaconu (6)
St Mary's CE Primary School, Credenhill

Summer

S ummer is hot
A round the swimming pool
N ow we can have an ice cream
D ancing on the golden sand.

Lily Townley-Taylor (5)
St Mary's CE Primary School, Credenhill

Summer

S and is hot
A nd the sun is hot
N ow I know it's the holidays
D own on the sunny, hot sand.

Imogen French (6)
St Mary's CE Primary School, Credenhill

Summer

S wimming at the beach
A sandcastle is built
N anny visits me
D addy takes us to the beach.

Ethan Clarke (5)
St Mary's CE Primary School, Credenhill

Sandy Beach

S wimming in the hot sun
A t the beach
N eed an ice cream
D on't forget your sunscreen!

Tyler Jones (6), Alanah Thomas (6) & Evie
St Mary's CE Primary School, Credenhill

Summer

S wimming at the beach
A sandcastle
N eed an ice cream
D addy driving us home.

Lucas Privett (5)
St Mary's CE Primary School, Credenhill

Sand

S andcastles
A nd it's beautiful
N ow I am on holiday
D igging sandcastles.

Laci May Evans (6)
St Mary's CE Primary School, Credenhill

Now Summer Is Here!

S wimming in the sea
A t the beach
N ever going home
D amp from the salty sea.

Michael Major (6)
St Mary's CE Primary School, Credenhill

Journey To Germany

A journey sounds like the engine of an aeroplane and the thousand wheels of suitcases rolling across the airport floor. The sounds of the scary toilet make me think the bathroom is going to flood.
A journey smells like sweeties and crisps, happiness in the air and the bad smell of aeroplane food.
A journey looks like a lot of happy faces and laughter from my family.
A journey feels like a cuddly teddy next to me and the hugging arms from my family.
It also feels like butterflies in my tummy.
It really feels like a never-ending flight!
A journey tastes like ice cream and Bretzeln and Amerikaner.

Tabea Gwosdz (8)
The Kingsley School For Girls, Leamington Spa

Furry And Cuddly

I am as big as a dinosaur
I am as cuddly as a teddy bear
I am as clever as a very well trained dog
I am as cute as a teddy bear
I am as soft as white snow
I am as beautiful as a Christmas tree
I am as smiley as a teddy bear
I am as furry as a teddy
I am as funny as a clown
I am as fast as a wild horse
I sleep as much as a dog.
What am I?

Valentina Gwosdz (6)
The Kingsley School For Girls, Leamington Spa

My Dream Holiday

A journey smells like delicious chocolate ice cream on the sea with tasty fruit smoothies
A journey sounds like a relaxing nap on the seaside and going on the aeroplane on the way back home and parties
A journey feels like happy faces on the holiday and jumping up and down with excitement
A journey tastes like lots of pizza on movie night and some sweets for a snack.

Maelann Rodgers-Jourdenais (7)
The Kingsley School For Girls, Leamington Spa

Furry Friends

I have a long tail
I have pointy, sticking ears
I wear a collar with a milk bowl on
I like people, I can stand on two legs
I can be a pet
I can run very fast
I have long whiskers
I have sharp teeth
I have soft paws
I have a wet nose
I have grey stripes on my tail
I feel happy when people stroke me.
What am I?

Alex Thorp (5)
The Kingsley School For Girls, Leamington Spa

A Beautiful Journey

A journey sounds like the waves from the sea washing to shore
A journey looks like a beautiful paradise with green palm trees that were blowing in the wind
A journey feels like golden grains of sand between your toes
A journey tastes like salty seawater in your mouth
A journey smells like salmon baking on the barbecue.

Kitty Sullivan (7)
The Kingsley School For Girls, Leamington Spa

My Senses

A journey seems like the really loud and scary toilet on the aeroplane
A journey looks like a fun and scary place
A journey smells like candyfloss clouds
A journey feels like a comfy seat with a massager and relaxes me
A journey tastes like sour sweets
I can hear birds chirping.

Liana Hanson (7)
The Kingsley School For Girls, Leamington Spa

Green And Spiky

I am dark green
I am bigger than a dolphin
I eat meat
I love a big mouth
I am enormous
I have big feet
I have a long tail
I am a bit fast at running
I have spots
I have a grey tail
I live in a forest of trees
What am I?

Juli Mueller-Piefkowski (7)
The Kingsley School For Girls, Leamington Spa

My Five Senses

A journey sounds like an adventure
It looks like waves on the beach
It feels like the hot sun shining on me until it's just right
It smells like sunscreen
It tastes like chocolate and sweets.

Lara Dolly Elliman (7)
The Kingsley School For Girls, Leamington Spa

Scary Guy

I am dark green
I live in trees
I eat mice (I catch really easily)
I crush bones
I hiss loudly
I am as long as seven streets!
What am I?

Lydia de Cates (5)
The Kingsley School For Girls, Leamington Spa

Jungle Animal

I eat meat
I am furry
I am as big as a lion
I crawl on four feet
I am as stripy as a zebra
What am I?

Elia Iyieke (5)
The Kingsley School For Girls, Leamington Spa

A Night-Time Friend

I am brown and small.
I eat slugs, insects and fruit in autumn.
I also eat juicy mealworms and beetles.
I live in forests and meadows.
I sleep in a nest on the ground.
Sometimes I like to visit garden sheds.
I hibernate during cold winters.
I can smell better than I can see.
My babies are called pups or hoglets.
Badgers are not my friends.
I am prickly.
What am I?

Zechariah McIlwain (6)
Tiverton Junior & Infant School, Selly Oak

The Creepy House

The creepy house is some rooms and you have to sleep close to your shoes.
Also, the creepy house smells like poo and stinky fish.
The kitchen smells like a garbage can with poo in it.
Outside smells, well... not that nice!
Finally, the bed smells a little bit nice.

Dano Najmadeen A. Muhamad (6)
Tiverton Junior & Infant School, Selly Oak

Dragon And Me

There was a dragon who was kind to me,
And he was sharing his cookie,
His name was Mookie,
We were playing duck, duck, goose,
And drinking blackcurrant juice,
He looked orange and red,
The dragon liked me as a friend.

Lucas Stasiak (6)
Tiverton Junior & Infant School, Selly Oak

Who I Live With

I live with my mom and my dad and my little sister and brother.
We care for each other and we love each other.
We care about God and we pray every day.

Joycelyn Asare-Bediako (5)
Tiverton Junior & Infant School, Selly Oak

Young Writers Information

We hope you have enjoyed reading this book – and that you will continue to in the coming years.

If you're a young writer who enjoys reading and creative writing, or the parent of an enthusiastic poet or story writer, do visit our website **www.youngwriters.co.uk**. Here you will find free competitions, workshops and games, as well as recommended reads, a poetry glossary and our blog.

If you would like to order further copies of this book, or any of our other titles, then please give us a call or visit **www.youngwriters.co.uk**.

Young Writers
Remus House
Coltsfoot Drive
Peterborough
PE2 9BF
(01733) 890066
info@youngwriters.co.uk

@YoungWritersUK @YoungWritersCW